VICTORIAN QUILTS

1875-1900

THEY AREN'T ALL CRAZY

Paul D. Pilgrim
Gerald E. Roy

Developed in conjunction with an exhibit at the
Museum of the American Quilter's Society (MAQS),
Paducah, KY, August 27, 1994 – January 14, 1995.

American Quilter's Society
P.O. Box 3290 • Paducah, KY 42002-3290

The Victorian Era was an age of opulence, a time when *more* was thought to, without a doubt, be *better*...

*A*s seen in everything from wall to bed coverings.

LEFT: MAQS installation of a period room setting. The 1880 Eastlake bed is constructed of pine and painted to suggest graining and inlay. Heavily detailed period linens
grace the bed, along with a Marseilles spread, and two china-head dolls.
Folded at the foot is an 1890 crazy quilt, typical in its embroidered fancy stitches,
but unusual in that it is made of cottons rather than silks and velvets. A screen to the
left is covered with reproduction wallpaper by Bradbury & Bradbury Wall Coverings.

ABOVE: Note in the full view of the crazy quilt that each block contains a recognizable
image in its center.

Collection of Pilgrim/Roy.
Dolls: Glendora Hutson; lamp & brass frames: Kay B. Smith; rug: Anthony Barnes Antiques.

$\mathcal{P}$HOTO CREDITS

RICHARD WALKER, Schenevus, NY
   Page: 3, 16, 17, 18, 19, 20, 21, 22, 23,
   24, 25, 26, 28, 29, 30, 31, 33, 34, 36,
   38, 39, 40, 42, 44, 46, 47, 48, 50, 51,
   52, 54, 56, 57, 58, 60, 61, 63

STEVE MARTIN, Henderson, KY
   Page: 2, 6, 7

CHARLEY LYNCH, Paducah, KY
   Page: Cover, 12, 13, 14, 15, 27, 35,
   37, 41, 43, 45, 49, 53, 55, 59

TABLE OF CONTENTS

$\mathcal{O}$pulent decoration and intricate detail were found in even the simplest of sewing tools...

ABOVE: German Black Forest carved bears hold thimbles and pincushions, and one stands on thread holder. A thimble and a spool of thread each have their own place on the silver-plated tray to the right. In the background, a silver-plated sewing bird makes several pincushions available and can also hold fabric in tension. If the bird's tail is pressed down, the beak opens so it can grasp fabric.

RIGHT: An array of tools includes pincushions, a lady's companion (an English travel kit in a leather box), various thimbles, a folding ruler, a chatelaine with various tools (meant to attach to a belt), a hole punch, scissors, a needle case, a glove mending tool, a seam gauge, and a wooden darning egg that holds a spool.

Collection of Pilgrim/Roy and the collection of Helen Thompson.

This was truly an era of visual delights.

ᛋNTRODUCTION

Throughout history needlework has provided a medium for expression and an aesthetic voice for many who might otherwise have had none. Quilts of the Victorian era are no exception.

Sewing skills were traditionally a part of any young woman's education, and were often passed from mother to daughter. As a young girl became more proficient, her projects increased in difficulty, so she continued to perfect her craft. This activity was often centered in the home, regardless of economic status. However, the projects and products often reflected a family's economic position.

For example, because of household staff there would be no reason for a young woman from a wealthy family to learn to make her own dresses. This afforded her the time to master fancy stitches and produce intricate pictures and complicated samplers, linens, and crazy quilts, all intended for show and decoration.

The craft of quiltmaking has traditionally provided an opportunity for involvement – a chance to comfortably participate and accomplish a practical goal and in the process also satisfy a creative need. Sewing tools and materials were available to everyone regardless of station, and women were very comfortable with these tools.

Time has always been a factor in the development of proficiency in any craft. Traditionally, sewing was a matter of necessity, and usually relegated to times of the day or year when more pressing activities demanded less attention. The most significant aspect of quiltmaking is that through it, materials that would otherwise have gone to waste were transformed into useful household items, and the labor intensive activity to create these items became pleasurable. Quilting may have been an important escape for women, and a means of satisfying a purely personal need.

The late nineteenth century brought many changes that affected an enormous number of people. The sewing machine was only one of many time-saving devices available. The Industrial Revolution had affected the broadest section of the population and created an enormous middle class. For the first time in history the largest section of the population found themselves financially comfortable. Many people took advantage of their prosperity and began to travel. World tours became fashionable; visiting museums, experiencing the luxury of hotels, and other offerings of the times produced a desire to incorporate some of these experiences in their own homes and lives.

Many families were afforded the luxury of domestic help, which allowed the women of the house to focus their attentions elsewhere. Decorating the home became a preoccupation with many women, and books were published on fashion, design, home furnishing, and decoration. The "New Aesthetic" was marketed extensively. Fabrics, wall coverings, and accessories of the latest fashion for the home were available to all who wished to purchase them.

"The majority of American homes belong to the great and highly respectable middle class, who by industry and economy have amassed moderate wealth, or are making sufficient money to provide their families with comfortable, and in many cases elegant homes."

Beautiful Homes or Hints in Household Furnishings by Henry T. Williams and Mrs. C. S. Jones. Volume 4 Williams Household Series. New York. Henry T. Williams, Publisher. 1878.

The travel provided nineteenth century middle class Americans a firsthand look at European society. England, a favorite destination for Americans provided inspiration for American style and fashion.

The long reign of Queen Victoria, 1837–1901, her enormous popularity, and her storybook romance and life with Prince Albert provided a fitting atmosphere for the period. Popular figures, they were often depicted by artists and craftsmen of the time, in, for example, porcelain and printed materials.

Enormous advances in technology provided the means for artists and craftsmen to mass produce many items that until this time had only been available to a privileged few. Many important collections were amassed during this period including those of Victoria and Albert, consummate collectors.

The untimely death of Prince Albert in 1861, just ten years into the reign of Queen Victoria, brought yet another element into focus – that of a grieving queen. Mourning became an art form that permeated the period. Art, literature, decoration, and fashion had already been affected by this "New Aesthetic." A renewed interest in antiquities coupled with affluence, romanticized by mourning, created a period of excess and opulence. The idea that more is better was the attitude of the day. No surface was left untouched. Flat surfaces became embellished with three dimensional elements or patterned with paint and gilding. Plainer surfaces were made to imitate more expensive materials and styles. Color was used along with gilding and faux finishes to dazzle the eye.

Needlework was affected by the "New Aesthetic." For many women, the crazy quilt or Victorian slumber throw became a means to incorporate many contemporary ideas and images in a decorative object designed to adorn the home. The crazy quilt was usually actually a tied comfort. In some cases the top was attached to a commercially produced quilted fabric by means of ties.

These throws were intended as decorative accents in a room. Very few were made to cover a bed. Most often small, they were used as throws over tables, pianos, sofas, or divans. When used on the bed, they were placed on top of another cover as a display. Most often these works were presented in the common rooms of the home. Made of silks, satins, velvets, and brocades, the heavy embell-ishments, painted motifs, and elaborate braided tassels, fringes, and lace that often finished these pieces rendered them very fragile and impractical.

"In England, in the most elegant mansions, the divan has become one of the principal features in home furnishings, and as the custom of adopting Oriental luxury is becoming popular among the higher classes, the introduction of the Persian divan with rugs of leopard skins and hangings of rich Eastern looms, is esteemed the per-fection of comfort and elegance combined."

Beautiful Homes, Chapter XV.

The crazy quilt, although it relates to quiltmaking, did not share a common audience or participation within the tradition. Many crazy quilt makers were perhaps people from other disciplines such as embroidery; people who were anxious to put their talents to work on a piece that would reflect the "New Aesthetic." The crazy quilt form introduces a technique that would not necessarily appeal to a traditional quiltmaker. The sewing skills necessary to create a traditional pieced or appliqué quilt would not be necessary to produce a crazy quilt. The idea of random patching of odd shaped pieces would be too unstructured for many traditionalists. The idea of combining any fabrics, images, and embellishments might prove to be too much freedom for quiltmakers deeply rooted in the tradition. However, we do see the influences of traditional quiltmaking during this period, and those pieces that incor-porate the "New Aesthetic" accompanied by superb sewing skills are those that achieve extraordinary effects.

Many crazy quilts may be the only effort of a single individual, which is very dif-ferent from the perfecting of a craft over time that is seen in other more traditional forms. In the crazy quilt we see a freedom of expression, the pure joy of creating spontaneously and emotionally without fear or encumbrance of a strict tradition and limited techniques. As has been the tradition in quiltmaking, anyone could partici-pate regardless of class or skill. Fancy materials were made available by mail order to those whose life style did not include their use. This style also allowed women the opportunity to express their convictions. Many pieces contained mementos reflecting the maker's personal, political, and social ideals.

During this period we see crazy quilt influences felt to a degree in traditional quiltmaking. Some quiltmakers were inspired to embellish their traditional pieces with elaborate embroidery stitches. Others chose to employ the crazy random patchwork within their repeated geometric blocks. There were also those who con-tinued in the traditions either unaware of the new techniques or uninterested in them. These pieces, although set apart by their use of fabrics of the period, are tra-ditional in technique.

The fabrics of traditional quiltmaking were largely printed cotton. The fabrics from the last quarter of the nineteenth century have an unmistakable quality and appearance. As in all periods, fashion dictates fabric design and color. Many printed cottons of the period are consistent in that they are called mourning prints, relating to the dark somber colors fashionable after Prince Albert's death. Printed cottons followed suit and reflected current taste. At this time manufacturers were also looking for ways to cut costs and keep their profits high, which was evident in the low thread count of the fabrics and the use of less color in a given design. The fabrics from this era are distinctive, and the quilts from this period are easily recognized. Often they are characterized as very dark with little contrast.

This is not to say that all pieces from the Victorian period exhibit these qualities. There are, of course, quilts from the late nineteenth century that continue to use bright clear color in keeping with earlier styles and tastes.

In retrospect, the crazy quilt was a style that burst upon the scene, made a noted contribution, and faded. An enigma to some traditional quiltmakers, the crazy quilt is viewed by others with amazement and esteem. Their nostalgic value is highly prized. To some they may appear slightly garish, but their surface decoration and attention to detail are astounding.

Historically styles have a way of repeating themselves. In quiltmaking we have experienced the revivals on a national level in the first quarter of the twentieth century, and the second revival in the third quarter of the twentieth century. It appears that even the crazy quilt is back again, reinterpreted with contemporary fabrics, techniques, and tools.

This quilt style provides for creative experimentation and pays great attention to surface decoration, combining any and all techniques, even to the extent that the finished product is totally impractical for use.

Victorian Quilts 1875–1900: They're Not All Crazy explores the different types of expression by quiltmakers during the last quarter of the nineteenth century. Typical and less usual examples are presented to illustrate this period of quiltmaking. It is our hope that you will enjoy all of these creations, and come away with a more complete understanding of the Victorian Aesthetic.

Paul D. Pilgrim
Gerald E. Roy

QUEEN VICTORIA
GOLDEN JUBILEE QUILT

Collection of MAQS – Gift of Sharon Hultgren.

Queen Victoria
Golden Jubilee Quilt

60" x 66", c.1887–1897
silks, brocades, velvets

Pieced using the English paper method (papers still attached), this quilt includes 149 pieced diamond shapes with hexagon stars and Stevengraph child theme bookmarks, woven ribbon appliqué, and woven pictorials.

◆　◆　◆

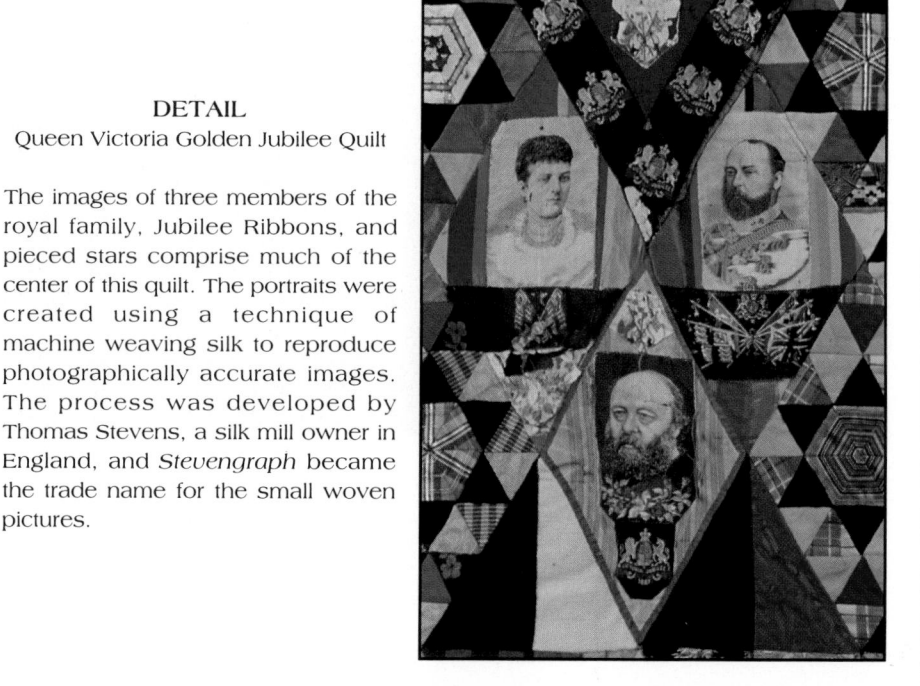

DETAIL
Queen Victoria Golden Jubilee Quilt

The images of three members of the royal family, Jubilee Ribbons, and pieced stars comprise much of the center of this quilt. The portraits were created using a technique of machine weaving silk to reproduce photographically accurate images. The process was developed by Thomas Stevens, a silk mill owner in England, and *Stevengraph* became the trade name for the small woven pictures.

CRAZY
COMFORT

Collection of Pilgrim/Roy.

CRAZY COMFORT

70" x 70", 1895
primarily velvets

The woven labels included in this quilt read "Dyer, Room 35, North 7 Temple Place, Boston, Massachusetts." Hattie P. Dyer, a milliner, was quite possibly the maker. The craftsmanship of this crazy comfort is so skillful that it was undoubtedly made by an accomplished seamstress. The border, with its intricately stripped velvets decorated with stitches, attests to this alone.

◆　◆　◆

DETAIL
Crazy Comfort

One of the velvet labels mentioned above.

CRAZY QUILT
WITH CRAZY PATCH CORNERS

Collection of Pilgrim/Roy.

CRAZY QUILT
WITH CRAZY PATCH CORNERS

69" x 71", constructed by Paul Pilgrim in 1990
using 20 nineteenth-century blocks found in California;
quilted by Toni Fisher.

The blocks in this quilt appear to have been made by the same person and well represent the style of 1886, displaying many of the varied techniques used in crazy quilts of the period. These 1886 crazy patch blocks were assembled in 1990 in a straightforward manner with velvet borders which showcase fancy quilting. Quilting would not have been usual for a quilt of this type. Had it been completed in 1886, the quilt would most likely have been tied or embroidered, rather than quilted; the center has been tied in a traditional manner.

◆　　◆　　◆

DETAIL
Crazy Quilt
with Crazy Patch Corners

Block showing the date, which was commonly included in pieces from this period. Attention to detail is shown in the traditional fancy stitches and in the bunch of strawberries so carefully appliquéd and embroidered.

CIGAR BAND
COMFORT

Collection of Mrs. Hewitt, Oakland, California.

Cigar Band Comfort

56" x 56", 1890
silks

Ruffled and backed with a fine Chinese silk, this quilt includes nine blocks set in three rows of three, each designed to display cigar bands in a unique and different manner. The center block is an especially dynamic Sunburst image.

◆　◆　◆

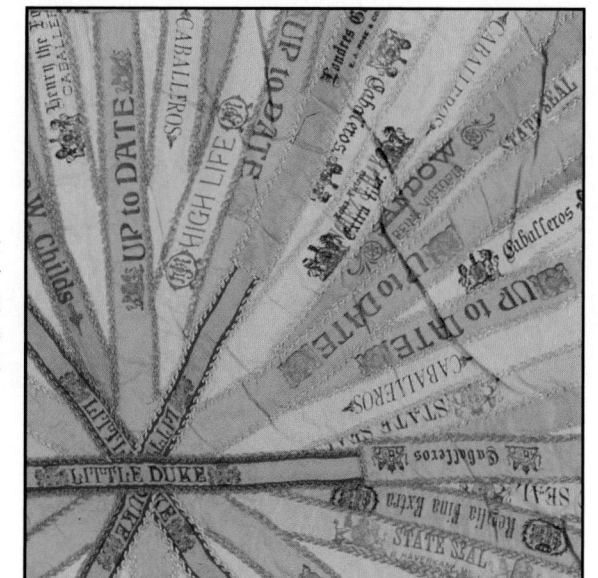

DETAIL
Cigar Band Comfort

The lettering in the Sunburst center block is carefully placed to create a balanced design and increase the graphic quality achieved using a limited palette.

CRAZY
QUILT

Collection of Pilgrim/Roy.

CRAZY QUILT

53" x 59", 1886
silks, satins, brocades, velvets, purchased cotton lace

This quilt and #6 are both crazy quilts that are typical of their period with their crazy patch construction, fancy embroidery stitches, and patches personally decorated and embellished by the maker as gifts for loved ones. This quilt is initialed "J.R.H./Joe from Carrie, XMAS '86."

❖ ❖ ❖

DETAIL
Crazy Quilt

Pets, initials, and nature motifs were favorite images for quilts of this period. In this quilt great effort was taken in rendering the initials.

CRAZY
PATCH

Collection of Pilgrim/Roy.

CRAZY PATCH

56" x 57", 1886
silks, satins, velvets, brocades

This quilt and #5 are both crazy quilts that are typical of their period, with their crazy patch construction, fancy embroidery stitches, and patches personally decorated and embellished by the maker as gifts for loved ones. This quilt is inscribed "G.R./To Momma from Carrie, XMAS '86."

◆　◆　◆

DETAIL
Crazy Patch

Many decorative elements taken from nature were used to adorn crazy quilts. Appliqué, embroidery, ruching, painting, and French knots were all combined to produce the effects the maker wanted.

CRAZY
THROW

Collection of Kathy Gellman, California.

Crazy Throw

57" x 57" with 4" lace trim, the Bish sisters, Pennsylvania, 1880
primarily velvets

This extraordinary example of the crazy quilt was made in Pennsylvania and then brought to Oregon by wagon train. The quilt is currently owned by the great-granddaughter and great-grandniece of the makers. The center is hand painted, and the quilt also contains ruched flowers, chenille flowers, hand-made cotton lace, and handmade velvet-covered wooden tassels. Family history recalls the Bish sisters wanted to make machine pieced and quilted works with their new sewing machine. Their mother allowed them to make the machine pieced and quilted Irish Chain (below) as long as they agreed to do one entirely by hand. The crazy quilt shown at left is the result of that promise.

◆　◆　◆

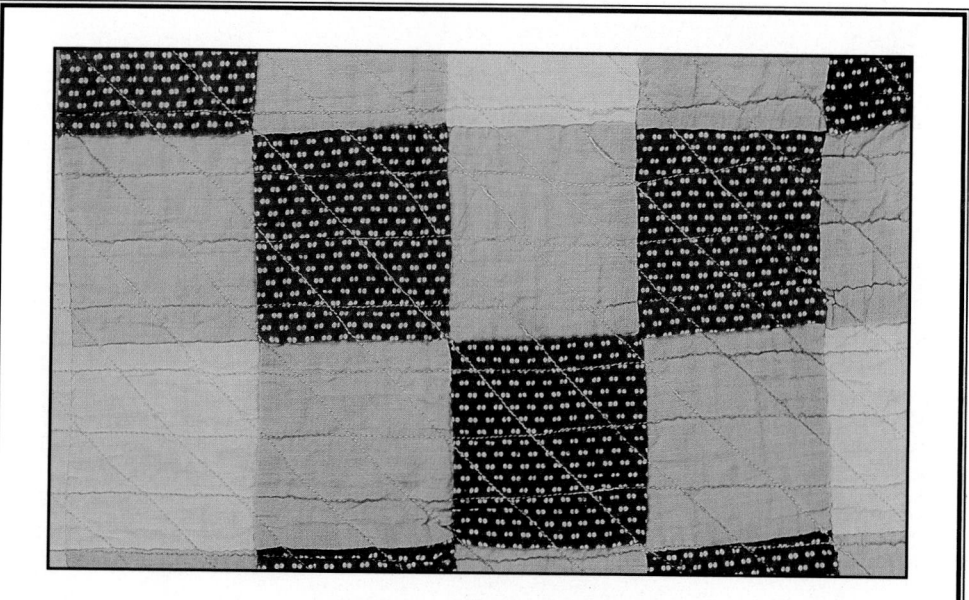

EXHIBITION - 8
Irish Chain, c. 1880, Detail

A machine pieced and quilted work by the Bish sisters. This Irish Chain quilt was red, white, and blue at one time, but the red is gone, so the quilt now looks just blue and white. The quilt has been washed often and the red was not colorfast.

Collection of Kathy Gellman, California.

CRAZY
QUILT

Collection of Glendora Hutson, Berkeley, California.

CRAZY QUILT

72" x 71", Pennsylvania, 1890
wools

Each block in this well organized 16-block quilt was obviously started with the middle fabric and built out to the edges. Each center area was then embroidered and each seam decorated with fancy embroidery stitches.

**BRASS DRESSMAKERS'
SCISSORS – German**
(Sewing Tool #39, Case A)

These dressmakers' scissors are decorated in an Art Nouveau style. The handles are elegantly stylized and the case has been created with great attention to detail; a utilitarian tool has become a very beautiful work of art.

Collection of Helen Thompson,
Lexington, Kentucky.

27

CRAZY QUILT

Collection of Pilgrim/Roy.

CRAZY QUILT

71" x 71", 1890
cottons

This crazy quilt is unusual in that it is entirely made of cotton fabrics, primarily prints. Only a few solid pieces are used in the entire quilt. Each of the nine blocks has a recognizable image in the center and the seams are embroidered in typical fancy stitches of the period.

◆ ◆ ◆

DETAIL
Crazy Quilt

The fan, a very popular motif reflecting influence from abroad, particularly the Orient, is one of the recognizable images used in the center of a block in this quilt.

ℜORTH CAROLINA
LILY

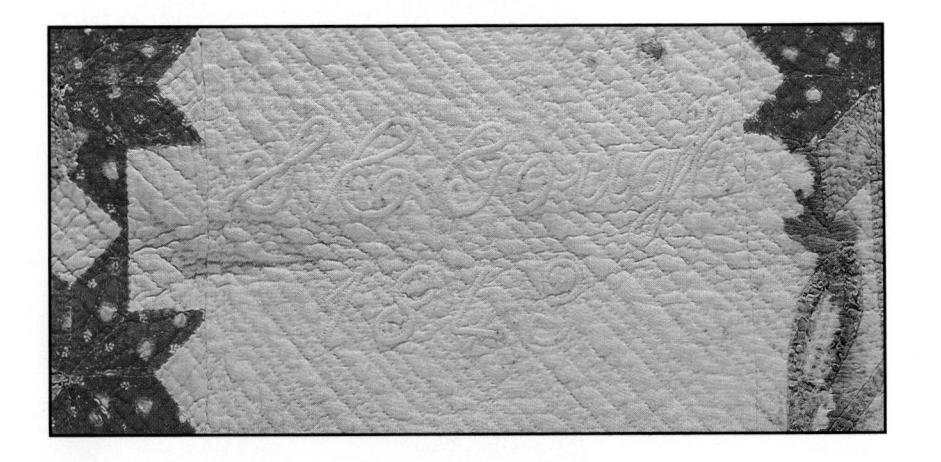

Full quilt and signature from the center block.
Collection of Pilgrim/Roy.

North Carolina Lily

99" x 88", Gough family, 1843
cottons

This quilt is made in the North Carolina Lily pattern, which was also called Mountain Lily in Kentucky. The quilt is signed and dated in the center block with exquisite quilting and stuffed work. Each of the alternate quilted blocks contains different original quilted patterns. Though it is an earlier quilt, this pre-1875 quilt is presented because it reflects the long continuing quiltmaking history of the Gough family, who settled in Logan County, Kentucky, after leaving Missouri. The quilt is in poor condition, but its existence, even in its present condition, attests to someone's feeling that it still has historic and aesthetic value.

◆　◆　◆

The next six quilts represent quilts made by the Gough family during the last quarter of the nineteenth century. Rarely do we have a chance to see quilts representing a single family's effect over a period of time. These quilts testify to the fact that in specific areas, i.e. Logan County, Kentucky, quiltmakers excelled. Many fine quilts have emerged from this area and we are fortunate to have these and be able to compare them. They are in unwashed condition, which may attest to the fact that although quilts were made to be used, they were also valued and preserved by families. Some of the fabrics in these quilts date before 1875. However, each contains a majority of fabrics from 1875–1900, and all but the Log Cabin exhibit the lack of strong contrast so commonly found in quilts of the late nineteenth century. These following six quilts represent a generation of quiltmaking from this family.

NINE-PATCH VARIATIONS BY THE GOUGH FAMILY

EXHIBITION – 12

NINE-PATCH VARIATION

78" x 86", Gough family, 1880
cottons
Collection of Pilgrim/Roy.

This Nine-Patch Variation produces the overall
effect of the Single Irish Chain pattern.

EXH

NINE-PATC

77" x 85", G
c
Collectior

This variation, whil
within the block, still

These Nine-Patch quilts, all variations of the same design, are a great example of what can be achieved visually by experimenting with different placements and color within a single design.

VARIATION

family, 1890

grim/Roy.

ging the proportion
ins the square set.

NINE-PATCH VARIATION

71" x 82", Gough family, 1890
cottons
Collection of Pilgrim/Roy.

Here the blocks are put "on point," giving a com-
pletely different appearance. Matching fabrics
give the quilt a sophisticated look.

Mountain
PEAK

Collection of Pilgrim/Roy.

MOUNTAIN PEAK

81" x 80", Gough family, 1890
cottons

Within the context of these available quilts from this one family, it appears that both scrap quilts and ones made with fabrics available in quantity or specially purchased for a particular piece are represented. This is an example where large amounts of two fabrics are used to unify all of the other scrap pieces.

◆　◆　◆

YARD GOODS
c.1880–1900

Samples of period yard goods, some still showing their original labels from the mills that produced them. By the 1880's there were more than 100,000 different fabrics being printed and sold in the United States. The fabric across the top of this display is a sample of Victorian period "cheater cloth" printed to look like patchwork – in this case to look like crazy piecing and fancy embroidery work.

Collection of Pilgrim/Roy.

$\mathcal{L}$OG CABIN
(BARN RAISING SET)

Collection of Pilgrim/Roy.

LOG CABIN (BARN RAISING SET)

74" x 86", Gough family, 1890
cottons

This Log Cabin quilt made with the Barn Raising set uses a striking combination of light shirting materials and dark mourning prints to insure its graphic effect. Green fabric has been carefully placed to complement the red centers, adding color interest and a particularly unique visual effect to this traditional pattern.

◆　　◆　　◆

WM. SIMPSON & SON FABRICS
From Eddystone Mfg. Co.

Swatches of fabrics available through the manufacturer. It is not often that such a large collection of fabric from a single seasonal promotion (Autumn 1889) is found. Note that Wm. Simpson & Sons recommended customers accept no substitutes for their goods.

Collection of Pilgrim/Roy.

ꟄIRDS
IN AIR

Collection of Pilgrim/Roy.

BIRDS IN AIR

74" x 90", Gough family, 1900
cottons

In this quilt only two fabrics, both from this period, are used for the design, which is used in an unusually large scale and set five blocks by six. With so few blocks and so strong a design element, one wonders what caused the maker to sew the last row of blocks on upside down. Perhaps the very close values so common in quilts of this period allowed the error to go unnoticed. In this less complex Gough family quilt, much less attention seems to have been paid to the design and to details.

◆　◆　◆

DETAIL
Birds in Air
This quilt's back is made of strips of the mourning fabrics so characteristic of the period.

$\mathcal{L}$ATTICE QUILT
(MENNONITE)

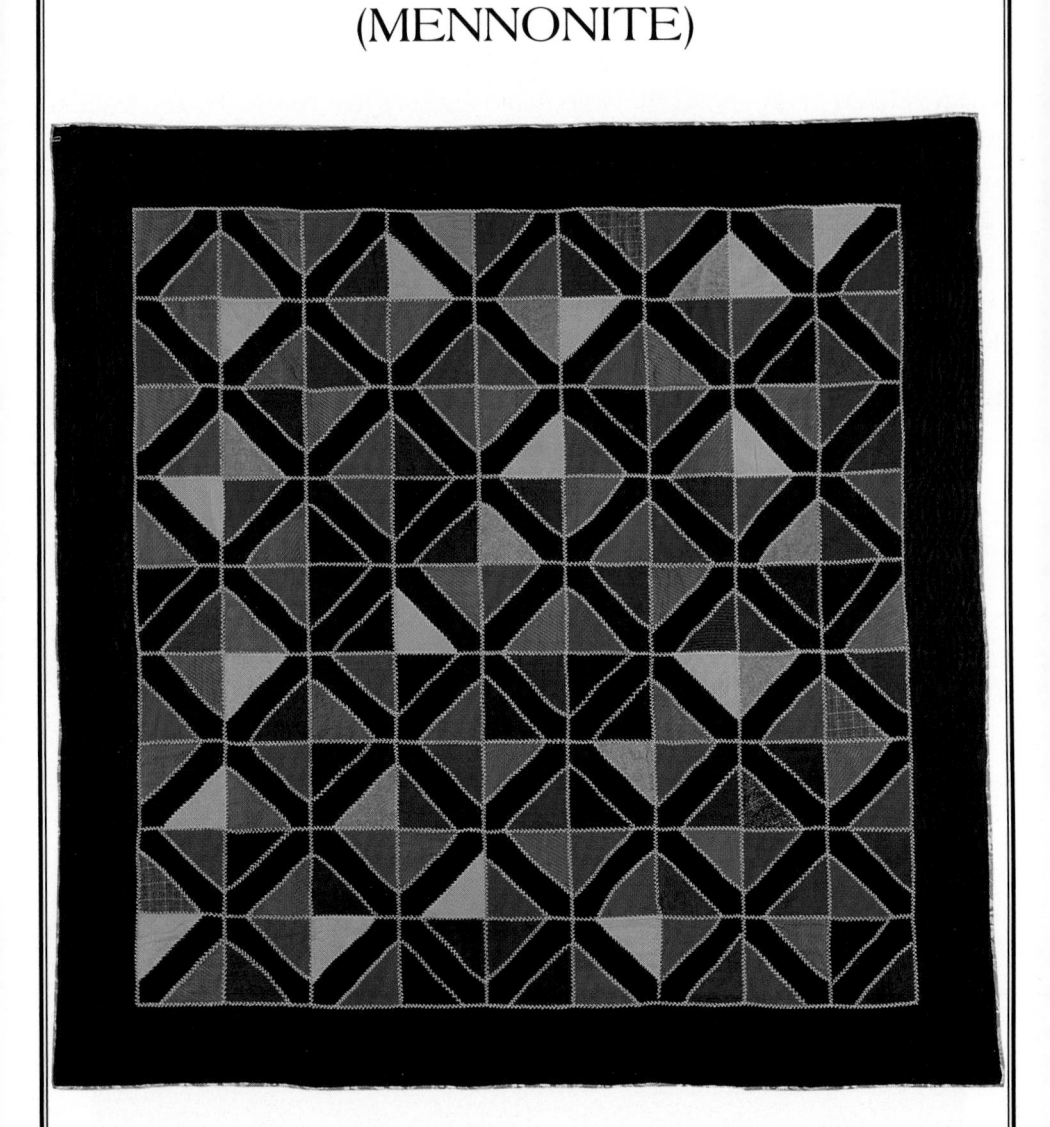

Collection of Pilgrim/Roy.

LATTICE QUILT

78" x 79", Mennonite, Lebanon County, Pennsylvania, 1890's
wools, silks, satins

Set side-by-side, each block in this quilt is divided diagonally by black, which runs between a dark fabric and a light fabric to create a very pleasing lattice. The overall design is further embellished with embroidery in the turkey track stitch, done in contrasting floss to give a linear quality to the design.

MOURNING PRINTS
cottons, c.1890

This is but a small sampling of the many "mourning prints" available during this period. These were fabrics that were acceptable for garments worn by a widow during her period of mourning. It is said that widows wore black for at least one year, with the color of mourning clothes lightening in value near the end of the prescribed mourning period. Some mourning prints incorporated small amounts of dulled color with the black.

Collection of Pilgrim/Roy.

$\mathcal{L}$ATTICE
VARIATION

Collection of Pilgrim/Roy.

LATTICE VARIATION

77" x 76", 1890
wools, silks, satins

The slightly curved piecing in the black diagonal of this block adds an interesting variation to the lattice design. The same color is used on both sides of the diagonal, giving the quilt a very different graphic quality from that of #18.

◆　◆　◆

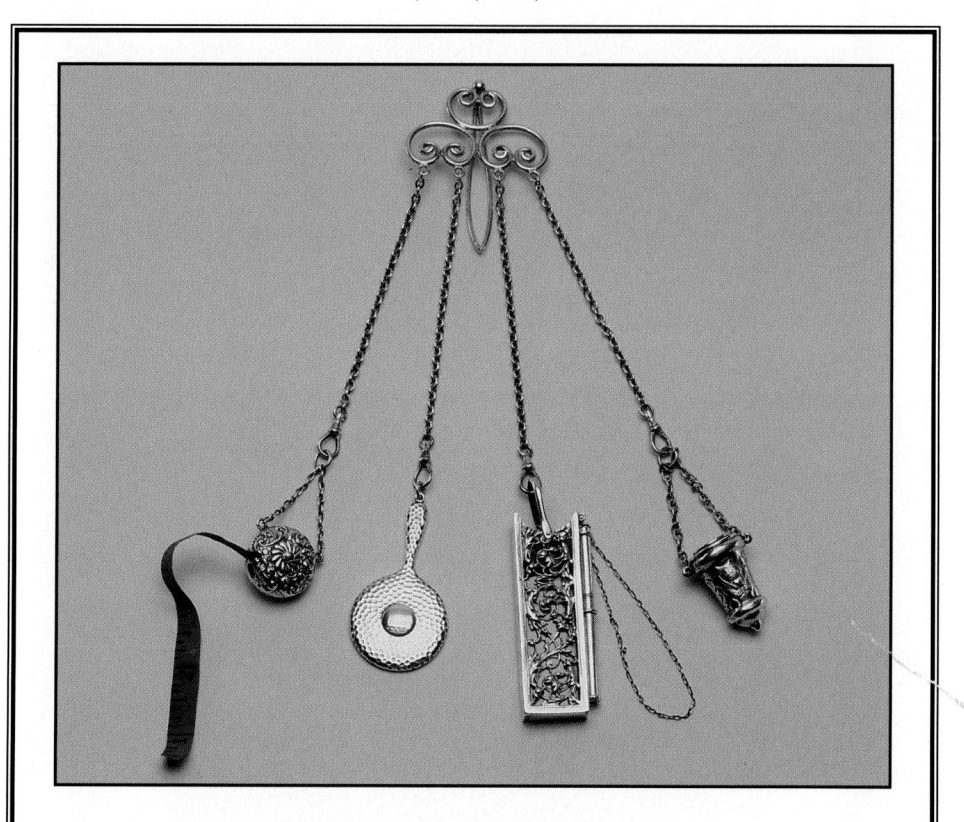

STERLING SILVER CHATELAINE
(Sewing Tool #1, Case A)

Chatelaines clipped onto the belt of a woman's dress and were worn to keep close at hand the necessary tools to attend to daily activities. Tools in this one included (L to R): a tape measure, hand mirror, note pad with pencil, and thimble holder with thimble.

Collection of Helen Thompson, Lexington, Kentucky.

CENTER MEDALLION APPLIQUÉ

Collection of Pilgrim/Roy.

CENTER MEDALLION APPLIQUÉ

70" X 77", 1890
cottons

The design is appliquéd onto a black whole-cloth quilted ground. A seamed backing was added, and all layers were bound with a traditional binding. This is the only example the curators have ever seen of this construction, which was perhaps devised for additional warmth.

The story that accompanied the quilt when it came into their possession is that it was made as a gift to an old order Mennonite Bishop when leaving his community to go to a new community. The contrast of the printed cottons against the black background creates a dramatic effect.

RIBBON CHATELAINE
(Sewing Tool #21, Case B)

Some chatelaines were much more modest than that shown on page 43. This one represents a homemade piece elegantly fashioned from ribbon to hold silver sewing tools. Included are (L to R): a strawberry emery with handle, a waxer, a pin/needle safe, a silver thimble & bag, and scissors. The waxer, a small spindle holding bees' wax, was used to draw thread through to make stitching easier. From the estate of Dr. Blythe of Paducah, Kentucky.

Collection of Pilgrim/Roy.

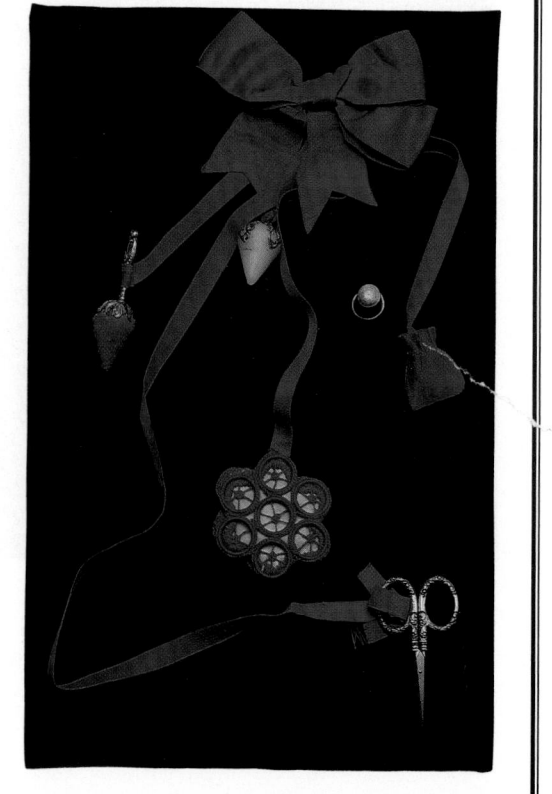

ROMAN SQUARE
TIED COMFORT

Collection of Pilgrim/Roy.

ROMAN SQUARE TIED COMFORT

70" X 71", 1890
silks, satins

In this quilt a woven effect has been achieved by the directional placement of the blue in one block and yellow stripes in the alternating block.

◆　　◆　　◆

ROLL-UP
(Sewing Tool #12, Case B)

Being very costly, chatelaines were not common; a more common way to keep sewing tools accessible at all times was a roll-up, often made by the owner. This was a continuous or pieced length of fabric fashioned to hold needles, threads, and pins. It was then rolled and tied or fastened in some way to be put in a pocket or bag. Pockets, although they had not been common in women's clothes in earlier periods, were well in use during the later part of the nineteenth century. A very lovely fabric with birds was used to fashion this roll-up.

Collection of Pilgrim/Roy.

ℬLAZING
STAR

Collection of Pilgrim/Roy.

BLAZING STAR

79" x 81", 1890
wools, satins

The strong visual impact of a star is usually enough, but this quiltmaker compounds the effect by adding fans and secondary star blocks to the design. The other elements allow the repeated use of white to balance this complex design. Embroidery stitches are then added over each seam to further embellish the surface.

◆　◆　◆

TYPICAL QUILT BLOCKS
1875–1900

The Schoolhouse block (bottom right) is a wonderful example of the use of a furnishings fabric in patchwork. The appliqué block is a traditional pattern usually found on muslin. In this case the Victorian quiltmaker choose to put it on a mourning print background. Two blocks contain "conversation" prints, fabrics with recognizable objects such as the boots with horseshoes, whips, caps, etc. These objects were most often printed in one or two colors on white.

Collection of Pilgrim/Roy.

STAR OF
BETHLEHEM

Collection of Pilgrim/Roy.

STAR OF BETHLEHEM

81" x 80", 1890
cottons, wools, velvets

This striking example of nine touching stars contains solid colors, woven plaids, tweeds, and wool twill. The strong visual impact of the stars against the brown wool twill is complemented by the exquisitely executed feather wreaths and fine crosshatched quilting.

◆ ◆ ◆

DETAIL
Star of Bethlehem

As is shown in this detail, this quilt is not only intricately pieced using a very difficult pattern, but also beautifully quilted.

FANS
(AMISH)

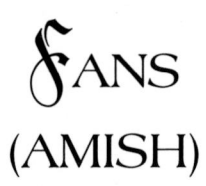

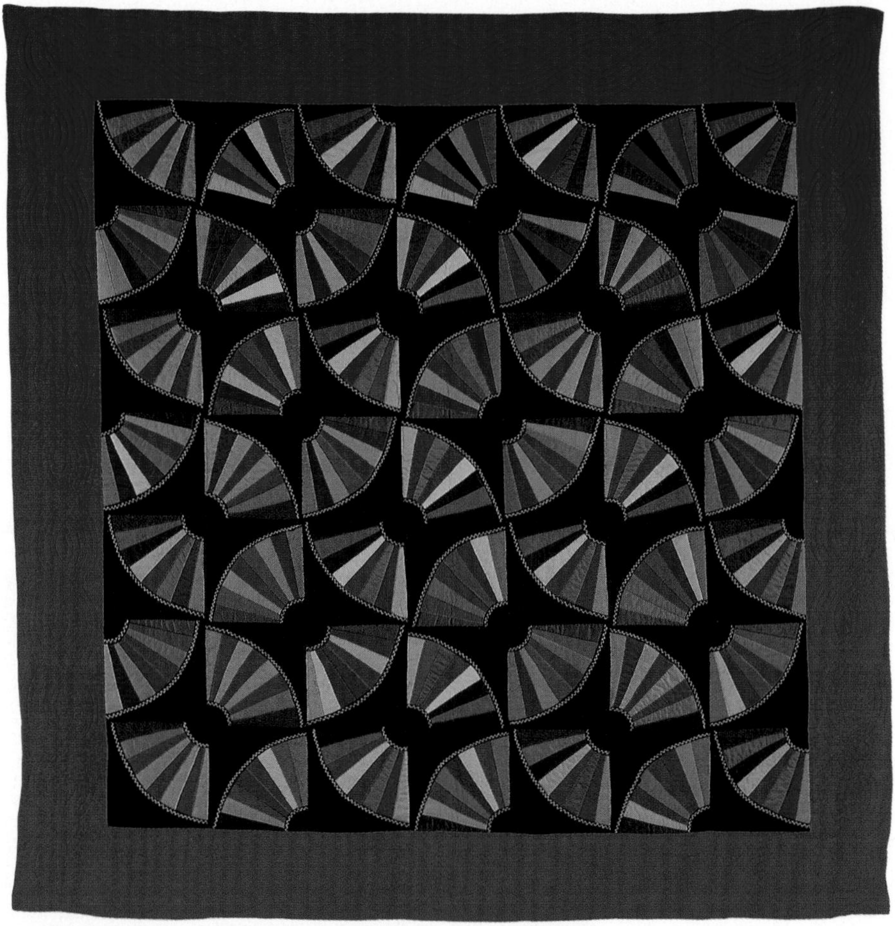

Collection of Pilgrim/Roy.

FANS

79" x 79", Lancaster County, Pennsylvania, 1900
wools

The strength of this quilt is the result not only of its color, but also of the set of its blocks. The design is accented by the restrained use of thick turkey track embroidery stitching only at the top and bottom of each fan. The serpentine lines created by this stitch travel diagonally across the surface of the quilt in both directions. The red border, with its perfectly scaled cable, serves as a fitting frame.

◆　◆　◆

MAKE-DO PINCUSHION
(Sewing Tool #13, Case B)

When a favorite item of home furnishing, such as a fine flint glass lamp, candlestick, or goblet, was broken, the base was often salvaged for use as the base of a homemade pincushion. Thus came into use the name "make-do pincushion."

Collection of Pilgrim/Roy.

ORIGINAL DESIGN
QUILT

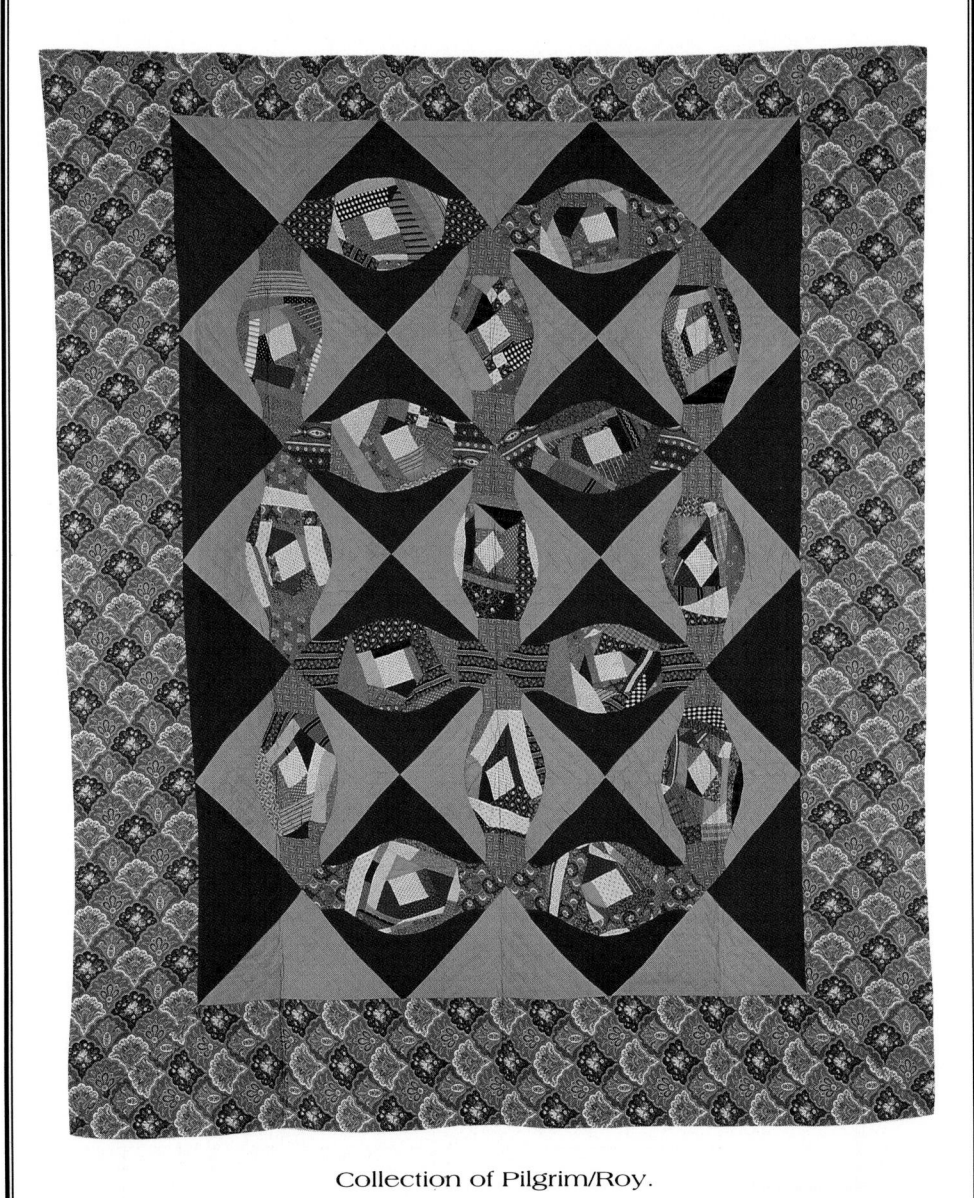

Collection of Pilgrim/Roy.

ORIGINAL DESIGN QUILT

79" x 93", Pennsylvania, 1880

cottons

This quilt can be seen as an example of how the random cutting and piecing introduced by crazy quilts influenced traditional quiltmaking. It is perhaps this new technique that allowed a quiltmaker the freedom to create this quilt.

◆　◆　◆

FURNISHING FABRIC
Cotton and wool, c.1880–1900

The fabrics produced during this period for drapery, upholstery, or home furnishings were very different than those for clothing. This is a small sampling of the fabrics and patterns that would have been available to a middle class Victorian family for use in drapery and upholstery. Note the larger scale prints in cotton and wool with more elaborate color combinations and designs. Often the patterns and colors in these fabrics were intended to have a rich Middle Eastern feel. Large florals and paisley prints were very popular. The lower right needlepoint is handmade, to replicate printed designs of the period.

Collection of Pilgrim/Roy.

CRIB & DOLL
QUILTS

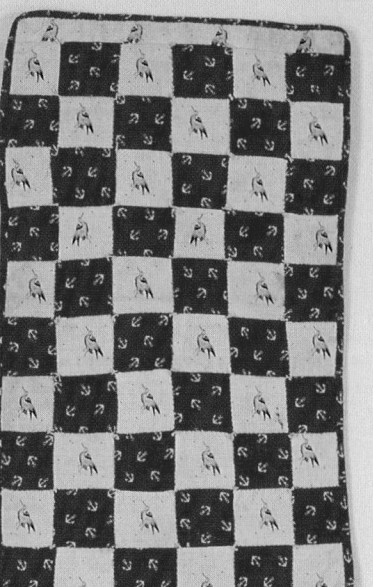

Collection of Pilgrim/Roy.

Crib and doll quilts are generally the rarest quilts of all; they were often worn out with use. The majority of the ones that have survived are cotton or wool. The very fragile nature of the silks and satins used during this period may account for the fact that very few crib or doll quilts of these fabrics are in evidence today.

OPPOSITE: EXHIBITION – 26 (TOP LEFT), 27 (TOP RIGHT), 28 (BOTTOM)

BELOW: EXHIBITION – 29

26 – COMFORT-STYLE DOLL QUILT, 11½" x 16", Paris, Tennessee, 1890, wools
This comforter-style doll quilt is a crazy patch, traditionally decorated with fancy embroidery stitches.

27 – ONE-PATCH DOLL COMFORT, 9½" x 16", 1890, cottons
Very careful planning has allowed presentation of one stork in each square. Conversation prints reached a height of popularity during this period.

28 – FOUR-PATCH TIED DOLL COMFORT, 11" x 19", Pennsylvania, 1890, cottons
Children would often be taught this pattern when first learning to sew. Their pieced tops were frequently tied during this period, rather than quilted.

29 – COMFORT-STYLE DOLL QUILT, 23" x 25", cottons
In this four-patch design, interesting red and blue fabrics that are typical of the period are used, and are set against a mourning print. The blues are in a family called "cadet blue." These differ from the indigo blues used earlier.

◆　◆　◆

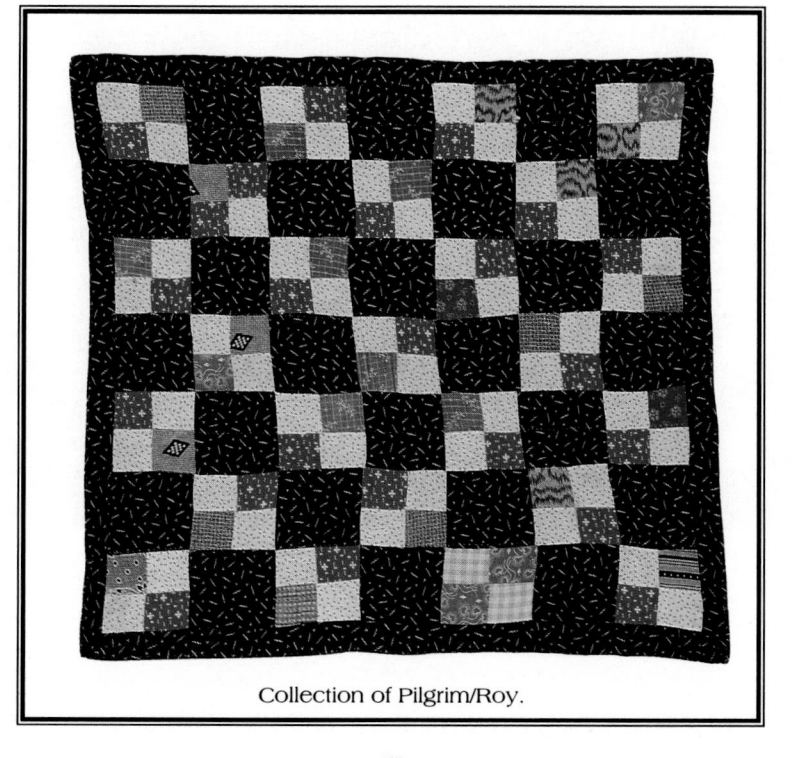

Collection of Pilgrim/Roy.

ᏚUNSHINE &
SHADOW

Collection of Pilgrim/Roy.

SUNSHINE & SHADOW WITH ZIGZAG BORDER

60" x 65", Rebecsa Gray, Lincoln, Illinois, c.1875
silks, satins, velvets

The work in this quilt exhibits not only this maker's ability to handle complex visual elements, but also her fine attention to workmanship. Quilt #31 is also her work. Her preoccupation with small intricate piecing is evident in each example. In a traditional Log Cabin of this period one would expect the pieces to be 1" in width instead of the closer to ¼" width she has used here.

◆　◆　◆

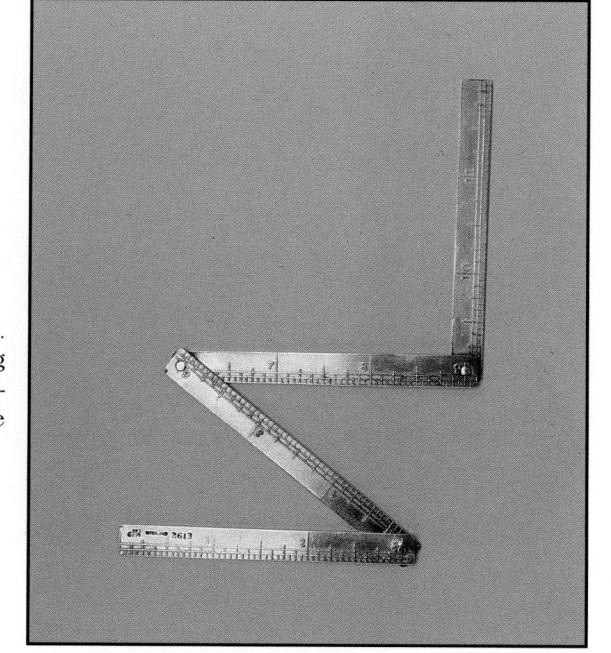

RULER
(Sewing Tool #16, Case A)

Sterling silver sewing ruler. Victorian period sewing items were made out of ordinary as well as very fine materials.

Collection of Pilgrim/Roy.

Mosaic
(TOP)

Collection of Pilgrim/Roy.

EXHIBITION – 31

Mosaic

55" x 63½", Rebecsa Gray, Lincoln, Illinois, c.1875
silks, satins

Unlike #30, this quilt is constructed using the English style of paper piecing. Paper templates were cut and each hexagon was turned under around the paper pattern. The papers remain inside each fabric piece, visible only on the back. (These remain because the top has not been completed.)

◆ ◆ ◆

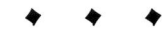

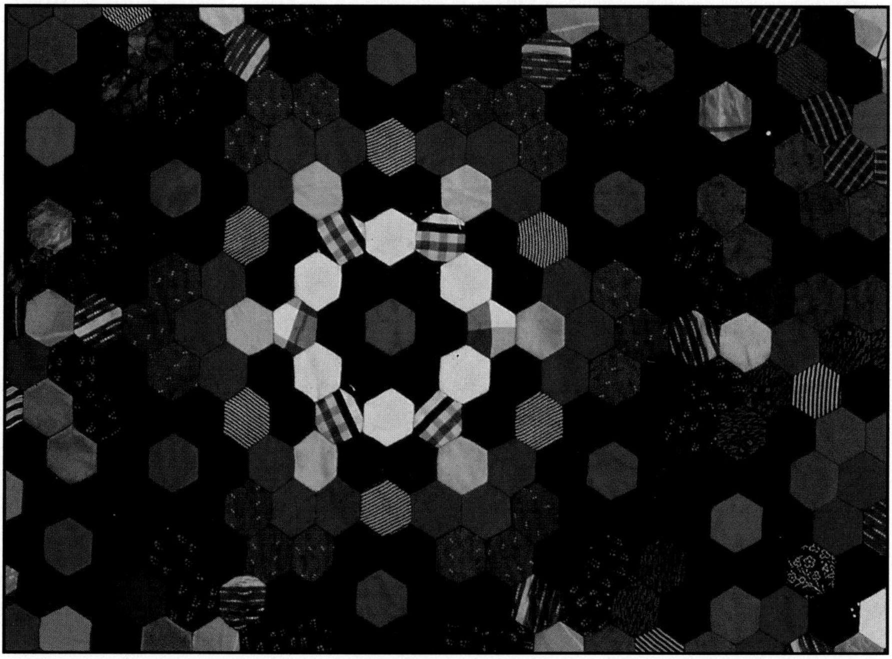

DETAIL
Mosaic

The English paper pieced hexagons of the mosaic top are so intricately stitched together the stitches are not visible on the front. Approximately 3,480 hexagons of fabric and paper were used.

THE 𝔓ILGRIM/𝔕OY
COLLECTION

The Pilgrim/Roy Quilt Collection began in 1972. Prior to collecting quilts as dealers we had amassed a sizable collection of Early American furniture, Folk Art, and Decoration. Although we had purchased quilts as decorative items for resale, it was not until we purchased the Herrick Log Cabin quilt in 1976 that we became aware of quiltmaking as a medium of expression. (See page 4 *The Log Cabin Returns to Kentucky* published by AQS 1993.) We then began to search for quilts that exhibited an individual style or personal expressive quality unique to the quiltmaker.

We came to quilt collecting with a fine arts background, and we applied the same aesthetic criteria to the selection of quilts as we had used in selecting other objects. Serious consideration has gone into the collection, and along the way we have made adjustments to control growth and maintain a standard of excellence. Collecting has led to many other areas for us. Being teachers, we naturally questioned, researched, wrote, lectured, and eventually chose quiltmaking as our own means of personal creative expression.

Today the collection contains some 2,800 items and spans 200 years of American quiltmaking. The earliest piece is a pieced Linsey Woolsey from New Hampshire dating from 1790. Our most recent piece was made in 1994. In addition to quilts, we have acquired items that relate to the history of quiltmaking. Blocks, tops, fabrics, and related sewing items and tools help to provide a complete and comprehensive collection.

One of our primary concerns has always been condition. Although we have been tempted many times by items that "were once wonderful," we have resisted, from the practical standpoint of storage. As conscientious collectors we want to preserve the items in the best way possible. We have had to make choices and focus time, energy, and space on items that warrant the effort.

While Victorian crazy quilts are in evidence in the Pilgrim/Roy Collection, they are not in great numbers. Because of the fragile nature of the most recognizable types of quilts from this era, few are represented in our collection. Most crazy quilts are in deteriorating condition.

LEFT: Paul D. Pilgrim (left) and Gerald E. Roy, curators. The quilt is a silk, satin, and velvet Log Cabin set in a Barn Raising Variation, c.1879, Massachusetts. Inscribed on the back is "To A. M. Herrick from her Mother age 81 1879."

No longer dealers, we are now simply collectors and curators, able to concentrate on specific areas of our collection and consult with other collectors and institutions.

Our involvement with AQS since 1984 and MAQS since 1991 has allowed us the opportunity to share the knowledge and pleasure we have derived from collecting. The AQS Appraiser Certification Program and our involvement as board members since its inception have allowed us the rare opportunity to reach many individuals.

The placing of monetary values on quilts has proven to be an effective conservation and preservation effort in itself.

We would like to thank all who have made this exhibit at MAQS and this book possible, particularly those who loaned pieces from their collections. Your generosity has allowed us to present a more complete and comprehensive experience.

Paul D. Pilgrim
Gerald E. Roy

MUSEUM OF THE AMERICAN QUILTER'S SOCIETY (MAQS)

215 Jefferson Street, Paducah, Kentucky

A dream long held by American Quilter's Society founders Bill and Meredith Schroeder and by quilters worldwide was realized on April 25, 1991, when the Museum of the American Quilter's Society (MAQS, pronounced "Max") opened its doors in Paducah, Kentucky. As is stated in brass lettering over the building's entrance, this non-profit institution is dedicated to "honoring today's quilter," by stimulating and supporting the study, appreciation, and development of quiltmaking throughout the world.

The 30,000 square foot facility includes a central exhibition gallery featuring a selection of quilts by contemporary quiltmakers from the museum's permanent collection, and two additional galleries displaying changing exhibits of antique and contemporary quilts. Lectures, workshops, and other related activities are held in the facility's spacious modern classrooms. A gift and book shop makes available a wide selection of fine crafts and quilt books. The museum is open year-round and is handicapped accessible.

For more information, write: MAQS, P.O. Box 1540, Paducah, KY 42002-1540 or phone: 502-442-8856.

OTHER MAQS EXHIBIT PUBLICATIONS

These books can be found in the MAQS bookshop and in local bookstores and quilt shops. If you are unable to locate a title in your area, you can order by mail from the publisher: AQS, P.O. Box 3290, Paducah, KY 42002-3290.

Please add $1 for the first book and $.40 for each additional one to cover postage and handling. International orders please add $1.50 for the first book and $1 for each additional one.

To order by VISA or MASTERCARD call: 1-800-626-5420 or fax: 1-502-898-8890.

Quilts: Old and New, A Similar View
Paul D. Pilgrim and Gerald E. Roy
#3715: AQS, 1993, 40 pages, 8¾" x 8", softbound, $12.95.

New Jersey Quilts – 1777 to 1950: Contributions to an American Tradition
The Heritage Quilt Project of New Jersey
#3332: AQS, 1992, 256 pages, 8½" x 11", softbound, $29.95.

Quilts: The Permanent Collection – MAQS
#2257: AQS, 1991, 100 pages, 10" x 6½", softbound, $9.95.

The Log Cabin Returns to Kentucky: Quilts from the Pilgrim/Roy Collection
Gerald E. Roy and Paul D. Pilgrim
#3329: AQS, 1992, 36 pages, 9" x 7", softbound, $12.95.

Nancy Crow: Work in Transition
Nancy Crow
#3331: AQS, 1992, 32 pages, 9" x 10", softbound, $12.95.